DNA RESULTS

DNA Results

Navigating Peaceful Family Dynamics

James Pehkonen

Amazing Life Design, LLC

CONTENTS

v

DISCLAIMER

Disclaimer: This book may bring up some difficult or painful memories or emotions. If you are struggling with any mental health issues, please seek the help of a qualified mental health professional. If you find yourself feeling overwhelmed or distressed, please stop reading and seek professional help.

This book in no way guarantees a peaceful relationship or connection with your biological relative. It is intended to support your life journey and is not a substitute for therapy, counseling, or coaching. You, the reader, are responsible for what you choose to implement or not. The author and publisher are not liable for any damages or losses resulting from the use of the information in the book. Thank you for reading.

DEDICATION

This book is for those who:

- are seeking peace
- want to do their best to initiate and establish a relationship with biological offspring years after birth
- have discovered biological relatives and have yet to build a relationship.

This book is dedicated to you!

PREFACE

This book is what I wish I had when I first discovered I had a biological son (and grandchildren).

It is not intended to be read from cover to cover. It is designed to be used as a reference. Some chapters are only relevant to certain situations, while others are based on specific stages in the journey of discovering a new relative of any sort.

As I write this book, I have been coaching for 20 years, 17 years as a paid professional. Most of my coaching has been in the realm of trauma processing and assisting people to create an amazing life. The foundational work here has been the transformation of how these people relate to themselves and how they can transform their experience of life.

With this book, you will at some level transform yourself. As you develop new and empowered communication tools, you will have the ability to assist the new people in your life to do the same and, together, create empowered relationships. The most wonderful benefit is that applying this work may transform existing relationships as well as new relationships. Enjoy!

INTRODUCTION

DNA testing has become increasingly popular as a tool for uncovering family histories and connecting with biological relatives. According to a report by the MIT Technology Review, as of 2018, more than 26 million people worldwide had taken an at-home DNA test; that number is expected to rise to over 100 million by 2021. The accessibility and affordability of DNA test kits have made it possible for people to discover previously unknown information about their genetic heritage and family connections.

A survey by a leading provider of DNA test kits found that one in three people who take their DNA test are able to find a new relative. This can include siblings, parents, grandparents, aunts, uncles, and cousins that they may not have even known existed. Connecting with a newly discovered relative can be a life-changing experience, as it offers the opportunity to learn more about one's family history, cultural background, and even medical history.

Once a new biological relative is discovered, the next step often is communication. It's important to approach these interactions with sensitivity and respect. It's essential to recognize that not everyone may be receptive to the discovery of a new biological relative, and it's important to allow others to process the information at their own pace. For those who are open to communication, connecting with a new biological relative can be a rewarding and fulfilling experience.

If you want to do your best to initiate, establish, and maintain a relationship with biological offspring years after conception and birth, this book and associated workbook are for you. Not only do you have to navigate the emotions arising inside of you, you also have to navigate the emotions of those around you, and understand the emotions of this new-found person you are DNA related to — and their circle of influence.

We will explore how to begin to establish effective communication with your newly discovered relative; I will guide you through the post-discovery phase, especially the first few critical weeks of the new relationship and how you can create a long-term relationship.

Together we'll navigate the steps to maximize the potential for creating a positive relationship moving forward. There are so many variables, yet in the end, creating an empowering relationship is the goal.

This book has an associated online workbook which can be downloaded at:
https://peacefulfamilydynamics.com/Workbook

FORWARD: MY STORY

I began coaching in 2002, and started a full-time career as a Life Architect in December 2005. Since 2008, my focus has been on addiction recovery, trauma and the human condition. I have conducted workshops for more than 30,000 people in addiction recovery centers and have worked with hundreds of individual clients.

On the morning of November 13, 2022, my DNA results came back. I had a 36-year-old son.

Let's back up: Two years earlier my youngest sister had purchased a DNA kit for me, and then I purchased one for her. When her results came back, she called me. Her first comment was, "There must be a mistake – the test says that I'm your half-sister." To which I replied, "You are my half-sister – everyone else in the family had the discussion for years that you had a different father. We all know that. You mean no one had a discussion with you? Your biological father is one of two men." I told her the names of the two men that might be her father.

When she confronted my biological mother about this, mom admitted that yes, one of the two men was my sister's biological father. It appeared that my younger sister did another DNA test and found she was related to the man that would that day be discovered to be my biological son.

Move the timeline forward a number of months: My younger sister contacted me and sent a picture of a young man that she said might be my biological son. I told her that most likely he was a relative (half-sibling) of her biological father.

In October 2022, my sister contacted me again and said that the DNA testing organization had determined the young man was from my sister's maternal side. It appeared that the young man was the biological son of either my late brother or myself. I ordered and took a DNA test.

Personally, I was sure the results would come back and I would learn my late brother had a son. On the morning of November 13, 2022, I would learn how wrong I was. My world turned upside down at 7:30 that morning.

My text is in black, and my son's is in blue.

Hello Justin,

My name is Jim and it appears like I am your biological father (just got my results back this morning).

I have mixed feelings, as I think you might also. I did not know that I have a child in the world …

If you want to reach out, know I'm here.

Thank you!
Jim
Sent at 08:06 AM

I am sure that it's a lot to take in, I know it is on my end, I had spoken with your sister last year but I was just so busy with everything going on in my life I didn't pay full attention to it, this obviously makes it clear. I always had questions on if Gary was my biological father or not since no one was on my birth certificate
01:22 PM

Thank you for responding. So my sister reached out already ... That is interesting.

Honestly I had no clue. Have you ever asked your mom?

If you ever want to talk, my number is XXX-XXX-XXXX. I'm open to talk.

I'm really confused why no one ever told me ... again, I'm open to talk.
Read 02:11 PM

Yes she had noticed that we were a match on here and we couldn't put together where the relationship was. I asked my mom before and she always just skated around the subject, how well did you know her?

02:19 PM

Real embarrassed here ... I do not remember her ...

What is your birth date?

You may not know – I had a brother and a few years ago it was discovered that Missy is my half-sister. So it was either me or my late brother.

Read 02:23 PM

I'll send you a picture of her, well I've lived here my whole life, graduated from high school in XXXX, worked as a mechanic most of my life but work as a manager of an auto shop now, have two kids, my oldest is XX and her name is XXXXX, my other daughters name is XXXXX, she is 4 and we just adopted her this year after doing foster care for her since she was XXXXX, I've been with my girlfriend for XXXXX years now her name is XXXXX, nothing too exciting

02:56 PM

That is so wonderful. So you are a mechanic!! I used to be able to do an engine change in under 4 hours!!

I had no clue I had gotten your mom pregnant – no clue at all. I had a few one night stands back then. Damn!! Still processing this whole thing ...

I hope you have no anger towards me ...
Read 03:02 PM

Oh definitely not, you were none the wiser so you couldn't have done anything differently, it is quite a shock even though I had my doubts
03:09 PM

Ummm ... are you going to share this with your mom?
Read 03:31 PM

I did, she said she did remember you
03:39 PM

Just talked to your mom ...
03:56 PM

oh no, I apologize ahead of time if she was crazy
04:00 PM

We knew each other ... dated a few times, and we were intimate once ...

She sent a picture, I remember your mom.
Read 04:18 PM

ok I just wanted to make sure she wasn't being crazy with you, she has a tendency to do that sometimes...
04:20 PM

She is in denial ... even though ... Y'know

I'm sure it is a complete shock to her.
Read 04:22 PM

I agree, its something I've had to deal with my whole life... she told me it's impossible but I mean...it's DNA ... it's pretty cut and dry lol
04:34 PM

What I think
Read 04:35 PM

I had a son. Less than two months after I turned 60. Single, two failed marriages — this was the LAST thing I ever expected to be a father, much less a grandfather!

In one of the afternoon messages, I shared my phone number with him. Within an hour I received a call from the biological mother. In our earlier communications, I said I did not did not remember anything about his mother, and most likely this was the result of a one-night stand.

The mother knew exactly who I was, the company I worked for, where we had met, the two dates we had, that we had been intimate once, and then I did not call her. I could feel the anger in her voice as she told me — seething anger. She said there was no way I could be the father. After a short discussion, I got off the phone. She continued texting for the next hour until I stopped responding. Each text from the biological mother came with further justification on how it was impossible that I was the father. She was in full denial, behaving more irrationally with each text.

Her son said I should block her. He told me he had never gotten a straight answer about who his father was. The box on his birth certificate was blank. The man who raised him had passed earlier that year.

In a text the following day, I stated I would never replace the man who raised him, and I did not want to damage the relationship with his mother. I was simply an "added bonus" in his life.

Tuesday morning, I began a search for supporting literature, podcasts, or books that could assist me to navigate establishing this relationship. I found one podcast, and one coach that specializes (mostly for women) in DNA results that impacts families.

That night I began this book. As a coach, I had been working with clients with deep trauma and addiction recovery since 2008. The first thing that arose inside me was deep anger. The story in my head after the interaction with my son's mother was: she has known all along.

The compassionate human inside said she was still holding on to the anger of my not calling her after we had been intimate. As I have no memory of any of our interactions, I have nothing to add. I was shocked she still had so much anger after 37 years.

Recently, with the ability to spit into a tube, mail it back and find out your DNA lineage has become so easy. What began as my sister and I each doing a DNA test, ended up with her discovering and me confirming the family's dirty little secret: that she was the product of our mother and a man other than the man who had raised her. She looked different from the other three kids, and had very different health issues. As a young person, I remember teasing her that she was adopted. My brother and sister would tell our little sister, "Go ahead and ask our parents. If you are adopted, do you think they will tell you the truth?" Childhood is rough, and siblings can be rougher!

Fast-forward to my sister reaching out to tell me that the DNA company had been able to say the match was on her maternal side. So this man was the son of either my late brother or myself.

On that day in November, I learned I was a father.

That day I learned it was my son.

As a result of having a son, I found little material on how to establish communication with this newly discovered biological relative. I sat down and wrote out what ended up being this book.

Establishing a solid and long lasting relationship with a newly discovered biological relative led me to writing this book. Let's begin by looking into the 10 Cs for creating an effective relationship.

1

RELATIONSHIP DEVELOPMENT

In this chapter I am going to outline the core principles I see as required for communication in healthy relationship development. It fits within step 4 of the overarching process, but knowing that people often only read the first chapter or two of a book, I want to make sure you get these most essential pieces upfront.

While many factors come into play, if you master these 10 Cs, you will stand the greatest chance of establishing and maintaining a healthy dynamic between you and your relatives.

The 10 Cs are:

Choice
Comfort

Connection
Commitment
Curiosity
Care
Conversation dynamics
Confidence
Clarity
Calm

By *embracing* these you will be able to understand the foundation of the qualities as you begin to open up communication within a new relationship as a result of the discovery.

Let's unpack the 10 Cs of Communication:

Choice — Empowered and empowering

Choice is freely selecting. To understand, we have to look at the root of the word decide. When we decide, if we look at the root of the word looking at examples like homicide (add in the other "cides" ...) something must die.

If you can learn to choose rather than decide, you will have more joy.

One of the things we have in life is choice. Often we make our decisions based upon experiences of the past. Once you understand that you either choose or decide, life can become easier to manage.

For many, the trauma and drama of early life will create the illusion (mental space) where it appears as if choice has been taken away from you.

You can do literally whatever you would like; there will be consequences of the actions that result from your choices. In order to create an empowering relationship, you must:

- come from a place of *being* committed to creating an incredible relationship
- be in the space where you are empowering other people to commit and "live into" their commitment.

Take a moment and read those bulleted items a few times to mentally digest them.

By making the choice to develop and create an empowering relationship, you will open up the space to do it, one communication at a time.

There is an important distinction between choice and decision. Simply put, choice is freely selecting something.

Comfort — Free flow of ideas and emotions

When you create the space to be comfortable expressing yourself, you allow yourself to have a free flow of ideas that empowers you to be free and connect.

One way you can create comfort, if it assists you, is to sit and meditate and allow your mind to clear. As it does clear, note the thoughts that may arise. If you have ongoing patterns of thought, write them down and share them with someone who can assist you to process them and allow you to get to a space where your thoughts free flow with joy and ease. It is OK if you're not comfortable closing your eyes. The goal is to notice your thoughts and allow them to flow.

Another distinction is explaining love and not-of-love. Love is the emotion each person is born with. At an early age, every human has an event that creates a break from love. Your not-of-love is a result of this early break from love. Because people have different life experiences, most understand love; yet that which is not love oftentimes is different based upon life experiences.

Not-of-love is not the opposite of love, it is that which is NOT love. When we experience the lack of love, that is what is not of love. If you think back when life gives you times where you do not feel love, that is the not-of-love.

Most people think the opposite of love is hate. Love and hate actually run parallel. Both have intense emotions, both cause humans to act and react in an intense emotional behavior, and humans will do incredible things based upon love or hate. The opposite of love (and hate) actually is apathy.

There are many ways we can bring our emotions back to operating from a space of love and creating comfort from the inside out. If you aren't able to do this yet for yourself, seek out a coach or mentor to help you release what holds you back.

Connection — Developing a bond

Any relationship has to have a connection. It may be because of something common, a family, the love of the outdoors, a career position, similar interests, or mutual friends. The development of a bond can also be done with certain interests that are not in alignment. At the end of the day, you are choosing to create a bond with another person.

There are different levels of connection: acquaintance, friend for a reason, friend for a season, the rare friend for a lifetime, biological family members, and those considered "family" even though there's no biological connection.

You may also have flatmates who may become common space family, sports activity friends, and those with whom you have common hobbies or interests.

Let's take a minute and explore "relationship." There are five levels you can achieve in relationships.

The first level is a stranger. This is someone you do not know. Most people begin as strangers, then, as they discover a deeper connection, take the friendship to a higher level.

The next level is acquaintance. This is someone you know at a surface level. You each may know each other's names and basic things about each other. And that is about all.

The next level is a friend. You share common interests, see each other and tend to enjoy each other's company. You do things together, and may share a common group of people you hang out with.

The next level is deep friendship. With these people you have a lot of commonality, and tend to talk quite frequently. You tend to do activities together. You share a lot of common interests. You consider each other best friends, buddies.

The deepest level is internal self-intimacy. This is the relationship you have with yourself. You may reflect on the relationship you have with yourself, and this level is where you accept yourself and have a high level of self-love.

If you are lacking in this level, it is an opportunity to engage with a coach to assist you to build your ability to deepen the intimacy you have for yourself. As you do this, you will be able to be with others in a deeper and more confident manner.

And remember, if you have a biological connection to the other person, that is the beginning connection to initially developing a bond. Utilize that and your intentions to develop a strong connection. Keep the thoughts positive and looking forward as you open the relationship. With each communication, you will develop and deepen the bond.

Commitment — Dedication through action

Commitment is the state or quality of being dedicated to a cause, or activity. Commitment is important in the development of a relationship as it assists to build trust and establish a sense of stability and security.

At times, commitment to growth and connection means letting go when you know something feels so "right" that it creates heavy emotion in you. If a situation has been created as a result of the discovery, create your commitment to respond from love as you foster the relationship.

If you want to develop a long lasting relationship, commitment levels will be critical. Commitment means you are creating the choice to be dedicated to the growth and development of the relationship, with the ultimate aim of creating a space of acceptance and love.

Sometimes we are committed to old patterns or ways which may need to be let go along the way. The most common thing to be committed to is that of wanting to be right. Now is the time to release this pattern. It will also mean at times, accepting others have a different point of view/perspective and we can still respond with love. Choosing to be committed to love and creating an empowering relationship will have you let go of the old pattern.

It's important to know what your commitment is: the relationship, looking good, or maybe self preservation can all be things to which we give power. Later in this book you will set intentions and goals and keep them in mind with each communication. This is how you can demonstrate your commitment and maintain trust.

Curiosity — Innate interest

People in successful relationships create a space where they are curious about each other and their lives. They keep that curiosity alive and a vital part of their relationship as they get to know each other. If you think about children, when a group of children get together, they have that initial curiosity and continue to learn about each other.

As you look to develop your curiosity, you may consider going back to the curiosity that young people have. Think about how curious young people are and the curiosity they have as they gain experience in life. What if you can create this space of curiosity in this growing relationship?

You can explore living in a space of wonder as you explore and develop this new relationship. Don't assume anything and ask simple questions

Care — Direction of flow/reciprocity

Successful relationships have a level of internal care that I'm going to call Sacred Selfishness, balanced with reciprocity from and to the other person. Do you care deeply about yourself, literally to the point of learning to honor yourself first and foremost? Too often people agree to things that go against their direction of flow, mostly for reasons associated with insecurity and attempting to be liked and accepted by others.

There is an old myth that relationships should be 50/50. This is a certain recipe for relationship failure. Each person is constantly judging the other and this sets up a scenario for failure. Imagine if you were to do a little more than the other person. If you do a little more, you begin to feel like they are doing less, so your mind naturally goes to judgmental, negative thoughts about the situation.

If you would like to develop a long-lasting relationship, imagine that you are responsible for 60 percent of the relationship and they are responsible for 40 percent. Ideally, you can get the other person to also agree, and attempt to be 60 percent responsible for the relationship with you being 40 percent responsible. What you are creating in this scenario is the space where each person is taking more responsibility than their "fair" share.

When you create this, you lose the judgment of "equal." As each person is taking mental responsibility for more of the relationship than the other, each person will end up working "more" than the other, resulting in a cohesive and empowered relationship.

Conversation Dynamics — The Art of Interaction

The way people engage in conversation, simply put, for most is a learned behavior. There are some who naturally have great conversational dynamics, yet the more someone practices "random conversations," the more masterful they can get at free flowing conversation with anyone.

As you develop your ability to engage in conversation, the easier all conversations will flow. The ability to create conversation often is strengthened by simply asking basic questions about the other person and then listening to their response. You can talk about the weather, a current neutral topic, possible activities they do or that you have in common.

We will go more in depth on conversational dynamics in Chapter 6: Creating empowered communication.

For now, it's easy to start improving your conversational dynamics by simply having random conversations with random people. I used to, in situations where I was in a long line, start random conversations with people about random topics. It is something that can really be quite fun, and with each conversation you will sharpen your skills in conversation.

Playing a game about creating random conversations will, over time, develop and increase your level of confidence. You also will learn to play and have fun.

Confidence — Being self-assured

Confidence means feeling a level of self assurance in yourself and your abilities, not in an arrogant way but in a secure way. Often a misconception about confidence is "fake it until you make it." When you fake something, your inner wisdom knows you are being deceptive and internal struggle occurs.

Confidence is created, nurtured, and grown. In life, we all have experienced trauma and drama as young humans that impacted our internal self-talk, and thus our innate confidence.

Building confidence has the impact of you being able to build and maintain relationships with greater ease. The more confidence you have within yourself, the easier it is to foster and grow a relationship.

As you implement the actions coming in the rest of this book, you will notice that your confidence will increase. THAT is the game. Confidence begets confidence, it will organically grow.

Clarity — Being clear

Clarity is like the weather. When your mind is clear, it is like a clear day. Emotions are similar to the weather fronts that come through. At times, the fog rolls in, or a thunderstorm rolls through, or rain comes through.

When a weather front arrives, clarity is lost while the front is coming through. As you go through emotions, it is similar to a weather front ...

You are in it for the duration of the weather event, then the weather returns to clarity. A clear mind comes back after every emotional storm.

Clarity is the space of being transparent in your thinking. Clarity can also be the space where nothing is in your conscious mind.

Oftentimes, in the moments when you first wake up, there is nothing in your mind, and you almost have to think to allow your thoughts to drop in.

Clarity might also be getting so simple in a thought that you create. Seeing where clarity is not there may look like where things are cloudy or confused.

Internally, as you develop a number of the other Cs from above and below this one, your internal clarity will increase. Life will appear to be far clearer as you process inside issues.

Have you ever meditated? This is one of the greatest things I have learned that assists me to return to a space of a clear mind.

A basic meditation can be found here: https://youtu.be/5saw8gWr1QY

Oftentimes, simply sitting in peace, closing your eyes (it's okay NOT to close your eyes to meditate, especially if you have had trauma), and breathing deeply in and out at a steady breath will quite possibly assist you to return to a mental space of clarity.

Explore ways for you to find peace in your own ways. What actions can you take to clear your head? It could be a walk, working out, journaling, listening to music, going for a run, calling a friend — just to list a few.

As you explore, see what works and does not work. Keep doing the things that are working. It is okay to take some time to figure out what works for you.

This increases our ability to approach life from a place of inner peace built on a platform of being calm, which allows us to create a strong relationship.

Calm — The space of inner peace

Calm is the feeling that arises inside when you have inner Peace. We live in a very chaotic world, which tends to have our life become very chaotic. One of the greatest things you can learn is how to bring yourself back to a space of calm. Know that the ability to calm yourself even under pressure is one of the best gifts you can give yourself in life.

Building this skill will not only help the relationship you develop go more smoothly, you will find your view on life shifts in a better way! We can create and make anything better in life from a space of calm and inner peace.

What three things stop people from accessing calm?

Releasing these can be hard to do on our own which is why it is so important that you find someone who has found their own inner calm to help you access yours if you haven't already.

Reflect on your growth in each area. If you are still not doing as well as you would like in a specific area, do some more work in that area. Our transformation occurs over a lifetime of work. Once something is healed, after a bit you will discover the next level of healing. That is the joy of the healing path in life.

Now you have the foundations of mindset in place, or well underway, you can start to follow the process to build a relationship with your newly discovered biological relative.

2

NAVIGATING THIS BOOK WITH FOCUS

You may just be starting your journey or you may be a little further along, it's okay if you want to jump to the most relevant section for you.

If you are not yet at a stage to take action, then you can skip the process section altogether and read some of the success stories in the back of this book.

The journey of reconnecting with a biological partner has nine steps. They are:

1. Questioning
   You may be considering doing a DNA test. Possibly to confirm a suspicion of a biological relative, learn about your genetic background, or you may have encountered someone who says they may be a biological

relative, but there is not yet any evidence. *If this is you, proceed to Chapter 3.*

2. Confirmation

   You have confirmation that there is a relative you didn't know through DNA tests and you are now wondering how you should proceed.

   If this is you, go to Chapter 4.

3. Choosing to initiate contact

   Once the news has sunk in, and you have chosen to write that initial message, learn how to write that first message.

   If this is you, go to Chapter 5.

4. Empowering communication

   Learn how to create your communication that empowers you to maximize the potential for an empowered relationship.

   If this is you, go to Chapter 6.

5. Initial online meeting

   After establishing and growing the relationship in writing, you are now moving forward to meet via an online video format. Creating the best you as you take communication to the next level.

   If this is you, go to Chapter 7.

6. Meeting in person

   You are choosing to meet up in person. This chapter will have you prepared for an empowering initial meeting in person. Being assured in your preparation is an excellent way to have the initial live meeting a wonderful experience for both of you.

   If this is you, go to Chapter 8.

7. Self reflection

At this point, it is time for some self reflection about where you are in the process. Let's take an authentic look at how *you* are doing in this process. This may bring up things to process as a result. You can grow through this process.

If this is you, go to Chapter 9.

8. Assessing the relationship

Let's now take a look at the relationship. How is it progressing? How are each of you progressing? Now is the time to develop an authentic assessment of the relationship, so you can both grow.

If this is you, go to Chapter 10.

9. Building a strong relationship moving forward

You both are choosing to move forward and grow the relationship. This chapter will assist you to move forward and deepen the relationship.

If this is you, go to Chapter 11.

3

CHOOSING TO DO A DNA TEST

"Let love always lead you to listen more deeply, under-stand more fully, connect more securely, forgive more freely, communicate more clearly, and respond more gently."
— *L.R. Knost*

This chapter is for those pondering whether or not to actually do a DNA test.

For your reasons, you are seriously considering doing a test to see if you can locate biological relatives that today you do not know.

It is a brave move, and you should give yourself a hand for choosing to move forward if you choose to do a DNA test. In the event a biological discovery is made, this will have a profound effect on your life.

Take a deep breath, maybe two and reflect on how things will change if, and when, a match is discovered.

Let's discuss three areas that may arise as a result of you getting (or simply contemplating getting) DNA results.

1. You may notice emotional turmoil arising.
2. Your mind may play out stories of what will happen when you connect with this DNA relative.
3. You may find a match, yet be faced with external pressures which may impact the quality of the relationship potential.

Let's explore these three areas.

Emotional turmoil

Finding a match may bring up emotional turmoil and triggers from unresolved trauma. It may also cause trauma as a result of not knowing you had a biological relative. You may also have an expectation that if the discovery does not meet your expectations, you may become distraught.

If you do become distraught, suicidal, or deeply depressed, please seek professional assistance. This book is not a substitute for professional care.

How is your internal self-assurance? Having a strong sense of self-assurance will help you stay steady as you go through this process. Let's take a quick look at this.

The higher level of inner self-assurance you have, the easier it will be as you navigate the waiting and the mystery surrounding this life situation. The lower your internal self-assurance, the higher the odds of a DNA discovery triggering a trauma response.

If you do have a high level of self-assurance, know this new discovery has the potential to be a fun and exciting endeavor. It also may bring a level of stress. The balance of this book has ways for you to be empowered and deal with the emotional turmoil. While you are growing and developing the relationship, please be gentle with yourself.

Mind creating stories

The mind is a very powerful thing. It has the innate ability to create stories, both good and bad. You may notice very different stories arising as you ponder what will happen once a match comes through. In my coaching practice and group work, we learn to understand the functioning of the mind to understand these stories. And the deeper you understand something, the easier it is to transform your behavior and minimize the impact.

Begin to simply understand that you create your experience of life based upon your past experiences, the perspective you have, and the understanding about how the mind creates this "reality" you call life. This book has some basic fundamentals in beginning to understand the impact of finding a new biological relative.

In the event you have a positive DNA biological result, notice how your mind begins to engage in "what if" thinking. What if we don't get along? What if I don't like them? What if they don't want to get to know me? What if they are just like me?

Understand that the mind has potential to take you into some dark places. In my life, the 10-minute conversation I had with the biological mom caused me to start to create stories, yet the moment I noticed I had begun to create stories, I could let them go because I have the tools to do that. Staying out of and getting out of dark places begins with noticing your thoughts.

External pressures

Finding a biological match, or simply seeking one, may bring up external pressures as a direct result of the discovery or even the potential for one. This book is designed to assist you in how you prepare for and create this new relationship, and how to navigate the external pressures that may arise as a result.

There may be very different ends of the spectrum as you embark on this journey. Some people may express great joy in the discovery while others may not want the discovery to the point of discouraging you or the relationship. Knowing this process up front will help you deal in a much more empowered way.

This step is simply a piece of the larger puzzle that comes with the discovery of a new biological relative.

Making the decision about DNA requires careful consideration. You are going to create an impact on your life. You may open up a chapter in life that you did not even realize existed. You may answer questions about the past that have been in your mind.

As you consider, take a moment, sit and let your mind clear. Ask yourself a simple question: Would my life possibly be better with a new biological relative(s)? If the answer is yes, proceed.

Whether you want to realign your current relationships before seeking DNA testing, or be better prepared to build a new relationship should one emerge, I invite you to actively do the exercises in the book to maximize the potential of your emotional turmoil, the stories in your mind, and external pressures *not* derailing a beautiful new relationship.

Most of all I want you to know you are not alone in this. If you haven't yet, please join the online community to access even more support as you go on this journey.

Together we can help you reconnect with: Let's do this! Let's create the strong and empowered you, so as you begin to create a new relationship, it is done in the most empowered way possible for the situation!

In the workbook, there are some exercises associated with

this chapter. Link is www.PeacefulFamilyDynamics.com/ Workbook or You can download the online workbook here.

4

DISCOVER A BIOLOGICAL RELATIVE?

*"Hope is being able to see that there is light
despite all of the darkness."*
— Desmond Tutu

Chances are, if you picked up this book, you have found a biological relative(s) outside your current family. And you are seeking to create a lasting relationship with them. This book will help you to create and foster an empowering relationship. Yes, you can do this!

You might have suspected your parents are not your biological parents. Maybe the "father" box on your birth certificate is blank and you have not been able to get a direct answer for why that is. Could you have been told you were adopted and are seeking to find your parents? You simply may be seeking vital medical records so you know your genetic medical history.

It is possible to find and create an incredible relationship with this new-found relative. Beyond this you will be able to fill that hole in your soul and create connection with this biological relation.

DNA tests have been around since the mid 1980s. Yet in the last 20 years, the popularity has grown. Since July of 2021, more than 26 million customers have added their respective DNA to four major health databases or with commercial ancestry companies. With each year, the chance of finding a biological relative increases. So chances are if you submit a DNA test, you may actually find a new discovery.

This discovery will bring a life shift. If you have discovered you have a biological match or new biological family member, this book is going to help you tap into how to build that relationship. You knew you were going on this journey; you've taken the first step. You may have found the journey is not as easy as you were hoping for or comes with more complexities.

Initially, when you are seeking a biological discovery, you were thinking that once you found them, all the answers would become apparent. What you're realizing is that may not be the case. And so now you're at a space where you are pondering this life shift as a result of this discovery. This book has been written for you because you have discovered a biological relative, and are ready and willing and open to establish an empowered relationship with this newly discovered person.

Know that there is a chance that this discovery may upset people who are hoping that the dark little secrets of the past do not arise to the light. Hopefully you are not like me: the biological mother is doing everything in her ability to convince my son not to create a relationship. I believe this is not the norm.

Chances are good you would like to foster and develop a very empowering and lasting relationship with the person or people your DNA results revealed. It is possible, and with a little work you can have it. The steps you take now to establish a relationship will shift your life and the lives of all those involved. The more thought you give to these actions before you take them, the better chance you have to create and foster an empowered relationship.

Let's begin with some self-reflective writing so you understand the goals of what you are creating in this new relationship. Take time to consider the opportunities that can arise out of a new relationship. It means not only getting to know a new biological relative, it means getting to better know and understand yourself.

Your existing family structure may be fractured, damaged, or wonderful. Regardless of where it is on the spectrum, you have the chance to create a new relationship, grow and develop that relationship. You have the opportunity to add a lot more people to your "family circle" that were not there before.

In the associated workbook, you have some exercises associated with this chapter. The workbook can be found at: www.PeacefulFamilyDynamics.com/Workbook. The link to get the workbook is here.

Author's thoughts at this point: This book may bring up some difficult or painful memories or emotions. If you are struggling with any mental health issues, please seek the help of a qualified mental health professional. If you find yourself feeling overwhelmed or distressed, please stop reading and seek professional help.

This book in no way guarantees a peaceful relationship or connection with your biological relative. It is intended to support your life journey and is not a substitute for therapy, counseling, or coaching. You, the reader, are responsible for what you choose to implement or not. The author and publisher are not liable for any damages or losses resulting from the use of the information in the book.

You or the newly discovered one may decide to create limitations on the relationship such as limited communication or not telling anyone on the discovered person's side because of the possibility of someone on the side actively working to limit or forbid relationship development.

If you need to know you are not alone in this and want to read some of the fears or obstacles others faced, and how they came out the other side refer to the inspirational stories in the latter chapters of this book.

5

CREATING THAT INITIAL MESSAGE

CHAPTER 5: CREATING THAT INITIAL MESSAGE

"The more you communicate love in your relationship,
you breathe new life into it."
— Elizabeth Bourgeret

A message wisely written can open up wonderful communication. Keep it as simple as you can. You are opening up communication. They may be expecting it or this may be a surprise. You could write up multiple messages before sending one, read them back and see which one sounds the best. If you know someone you trust to review what you have written, you may ask them to read and recommend which message sounds like it comes from the heart.

Write the message from a place of love. When you open with an intention of the heart, that energetic message will be felt by the one receiving it. The person reading it should feel the love.

As you review potential messages, imagine which one will create a smile on their face. You will begin the relationship by causing a feeling of love and acceptance. Imagine how you would feel receiving this message. If you feel the intended love, that is good! You are beginning to build a long-term relationship one message at a time.

Understand they may choose not to respond for a number of reasons. As disappointing as this will be, for reasons known or unknown, they may choose to remain silent.

This silence may be short term or you may not ever get a response. Quite possibly they are processing what has occurred or might be figuring out how the situation will fit in their life. Patience is the key here.

If results were through a DNA company, quite possibly they are no longer active or may have changed their email and not updated their email address. You should be able to see if the message has been received and when it was received.

Through the initial communication, you may learn they have external pressures from their relatives who are against them forming a relationship with you. With this one, you may experience times of silence between you and your new relative. Be patience and allow this person to process and grow the relationship at a mutually accepted pace. If you are texting with them, you may instantly text them, and they may take a while to respond or vice-versa. Keep in mind, finding a level of patience as the relationship grows will keep the communication channels open.

They also may be processing what is happening, so it is essential to create a space of peace and presence to keep a level head. Sometimes the development of a relationship may take what you think is an excessive amount of time. That is okay. That old saying, "patience is a virtue" kicks in here. Reflect on that and allow the time it takes to create and grow this relationship.

The saddest potential situation is finding out this biological relative has passed. While it may close the door, you might be able to reach out to some of their relatives, connect and learn about the passed relative through those who knew them.

In the associated workbook, you have some exercises associated with this chapter. The workbook can be found at: www.PeacefulFamilyDynamics.com/Workbook. The link to get the workbook is here.

6

ONGOING COMMUNICATION

"Honest, open communication is the only street that leads us into the real world ... We then begin to grow as never before. And once we are on this road, happiness cannot be far away."
— John Joseph Powell

This section will assist you in creating open, positive communications and addressing your mental stories in the event it is not opening up as you expect.

Now that communication has been opened up, how do you move forward in an empowering way so as to grow the relationship? This relationship has so much potential. Finding family that you didn't know existed can be a wonderful and exciting time.

The early communication steps are crucial to creating a solid foundation. Being empowered with your intentions in mind will help you stay on a positive track as the relationship develops. By writing out your intentions, you will deepen the relationship.

As you continue to communicate, focus on your intention with each message. Is what you are communicating in line with the intention you have created for the relationship?

What is your level of confidence that you can successfully do this? If you lack confidence or are insecure, you may create messaging that are not effective or in alignment with your commitments. Confidence is a state of mind that takes a while to build up if it is an area you struggle with in life.

There is a section in this book that has the 10 Cs of effective communication. So if you are struggling with confidence, refer back to chapter 1 to develop it.

Let's look at a few common issues that arise in this stage of relationship development.

Open communication occurs when your communication is intentional and steady. Reflecting upon the intentions you created in the last chapter for the relationship will keep your focus on the growth of the relationship. Each communication builds upon the last.

In your early communications, avoid politics, religion, and other comments that would be considered not appropriate. We live in a time where there is great division in our society, including the impact of the pandemic on our psyche. Remember, you are creating and building a relationship, that is your primary objective.

They may say something that upsets you. You may say something that inadvertently upsets them. Caution in the first stages is very important. Although you cannot anticipate every possible reaction, keeping things neutral and reflecting upon your commitment as you are writing will keep the relationship moving forward.

If something is written that upsets you, ask yourself one question: At the end of the day, is the feeling of internal upset enough to derail the relationship? This is a good place to learn about your emotional reactivity. While you may feel as though a comment is a personal attack, understand that most likely this "attack" is very likely your interpretation and is not the intention of the other person. At this point, choose to be in the space of love and understanding.

You will find that chances are you cannot get upset to the point that warrants terminating the relationship.

Relationship development is so unique. One may want to meet before the other is ready. You do not know what the other person is going through as they are establishing the relationship. They (or you) may have some reason to be cautious as you establish a relationship. There also may be external factors in play that could be impacting the speed of getting to know each other. Be patient and you will be rewarded with the perfect time to take it to the next level.

Some of the common struggles that tend to arise during the early communications include telling yourself stories about why they do not communicate back. The best thing is to develop patience and breathe. Allow the other person to take the time they need to reach back to you. If you instantly respond to each communication, that may inadvertently create stress for them. Let the stories you create go and patiently wait for a response.

Humans often create meaning when they read into communications and what they make it mean does not match the intentions of the other person. People might say things that trigger you, creating meaning that was never intended to be there. Remember, other people also are navigating situations the best they can. Having patience and not reading into communications is critical.

Once you have your intentions written, you can review them before you write the message or after you write the message but before you send it. If you tend to over analyze, it is quite natural to bring your analytical tendency with you as you review what you have written. If you realize you are overanalyzing, simply take a break, go for a walk, at minimum take some deep breaths.

Write the message, review it, and send it off to them.

If you are putting undue pressure on them to take the relationship to a place they are not ready for, they will push you away or withdraw. And as they do, you might get panicked and get more aggressive in your communication. Understand how this behavior will push them away.

Relationships will develop naturally when other people have similar goals and you are coming from a place of peace, patience, and love.

In the associated workbook, you have some exercises associated with this chapter. The workbook can be found at: www.PeacefulFamilyDynamics.com/Workbook. The link to get the workbook is here.

7

ONLINE MEETING PREP

"We think we meet someone with our eyes
But we actually meet them with our soul."
— Mimi Novic

Congratulations, an initial online first meeting is in the works. You are powerfully taking your relationship to the next step. As with the written communication, planning for success will create a successful first meeting. So again, we are going to create a plan and create the space for this meeting to succeed.

As you prepare, some initial questions may arise that will have you ponder as you prepare. Your preparation is key. If you choose not to prepare, you are minimizing the potential for success.

This is where you come back to your intentions for the relationship. The guidelines were in chapter 4, and have exercises in the online workbook. If you skipped that chapter and aren't clear on your intentions, please read it and set your intentions now.

In the workbook, there are some exercises associated with this chapter. The workbook can be found at: www.PeacefulFamilyDynamics.com/Workbook. You can download the online workbook here.

Review your intentions and journal within the workbook what you might expect as a result of your first online meeting. What if you created a clear intention that you could *expect* to have a great meeting? What if you created the expectation that as a result of the interaction, you two will be drawn close? Doing some work up front will increase the chance of a successful first meeting.

Also, remember the other person likely also has fears and a level of uncertainty. They may be nervous and have some fears about this next step. That is quite normal. Understand that the fears are there, as is the possibility of creating a wonderful first meeting.

Notice where your mental focus is as you prepare for your first meeting. It is very normal to focus on the negative. It is natural for humans to focus on the negative because the survival mechanism kicks in. And once you begin to focus on the negative, your mind will literally "spin out" and create more and more and more negative mental scenarios.

The game becomes "seeing" when you go into a negative head space and noticing how your mind will bring up similar negative events that could go wrong. Take a breath, maybe two. Deeply breathe in and let the negative thoughts go. Please note this sounds easy, yet the actual practice takes practice and perseverance. If you're new to this concept, start with a nice, deep breath.

Let's focus on what just might go right. Notice where your mental focus is. Chances are if you have agreed to meet, you are both at some level looking forward to the meeting. Quite possibly it can all go right. One or both of you might be a little nervous, you may have initial stumbles, but never lose sight of the fact that you are a Spiritual Being having a human experience.

The entire call may go right. What if you have this thought in your mind? What if your mindset became: this call can actually go right? That it is going to be a wonderful experience, and you will both succeed in the next step! Notice how you "feel" when your mindset is positive, or at least when you have more time being positive than being negative.

Time to prepare for success. Take some deep breaths. Reflect upon your intention for developing this relationship. Create an empowered mindset that this is going to be a positive step toward the relationship you are developing. You can do this! You *will* do this. Prepare from the space of *knowing* you can do this.

It sounds simple, but what I've learned in over 20 years of coaching is staying in a positive mindset takes work. This is not an easy practice to master, yet the more you practice, the easier this practice becomes. A great place to start is simply noticing your thoughts.

Create a mindset of confidence, clarity, and love. You may have some internal struggles in your mind as you think and prepare for the meeting. These are normal, almost expected. We are going to explore a few of the struggles that may arise during preparation.

Drop the desire to do this perfectly. The impetus to do it "perfect" is the mind's way of twisting you into a negative space. Give yourself permission to *not* be perfect. Give yourself permission to be you, as perfect and imperfect as you are. What if you choose to be authentic and genuinely you? Simply be yourself. Bring all of you to this first meeting.

As discussed before, the shadow side of your mind may attempt to undermine the confidence you bring into this first call. If you pay attention to your mind, you will see you most likely float in and out of "confidence" as time leads up to the first call. When you can begin to accept that you most likely will float in and out of this confidence state, then you know that you are quite normal. Can you accept that you flow in and out of a state of ideal confidence? I highly recommend practicing this before you get on the call. Start to notice when this happens at work, in the store or other low-pressure places.

Pressure to avoid rejection, stepping over your own needs may arise. Rejection happens. In spite of all the best preparation, rejection will always be a possibility. Yet with the proper preparation, the chances of rejection go way down. Noticing the thoughts that create these pressures will allow you to choose to step into your intention and goals, and minimize the potential of rejection.

As much as pressure is natural, the more you understand it is an internally created state of being. And with some awareness, you can learn to see it, and let it go.

You may be bringing past failures into the call. There is an aspect of self-sabotage to this, and it has the potential to allow those failures to cause yet another failure. We all have internal triggers, and with stress and the anxiety that may arise, these internal triggers may get activated. When you notice a trigger arising within you, simply begin to see it arising, acknowledge it and let it go.

There is no reason to bring any past failures into this call. This is a brand-new interaction, and with the preparation you have done, you can let past failures go. Step into the potential that your past failures will actually stay in your past. This call is going to have a high potential for success. Period.

Live as if THAT is your truth.

Select the clothes you'll wear and consider your background with the mindset of success. Wear clothes you are most comfortable wearing. You don't have to wear a formal outfit, nor should you be in your pajamas. Prepare to be comfortable. Have your background look and feel inviting (avoid political slogans or any other societal triggers that are not fairly neutral).

Consider using the backdrop of your online service. You may want to blur the background, or even use a virtual background. Or pick a background that is neutral. Just create something that you are comfortable with. The simpler the better.

Create a checklist that will assure the highest probability of success. Focus on your intentions for the relationship. In the workbook, there are some exercises associated with this chapter. The workbook can be found at: www.PeacefulFamilyDynamics.com/Workbook. You can download the online workbook here.

Here you will create an outline for the call. Write down the key talking points, which will then become your *guide* during the call. The call may follow it, or it may deviate from it.

Know that the call will be exactly what it is. Yet if you create and follow a guideline, the chance of it becoming a memorable and positive event will increase. And at the end of the day, *that* is the best preparation you can do.

8

THE FIRST MEETING

"All first meetings go like this:
Be open. Be honest.
What is it you do when I am not around?
Where is it you come from?
Don't dance around questions. Tell me."
— Ezinne Orjiako, Nkem

Most likely as a result of a great virtual meeting, a face-to-face meeting is being planned. You are taking it to the next level — to actually meet face to face. As you have had success up to date, time to plan for continued success.

Let's begin by looking at possible questions that may arise as you prepare for that first face-to-face meeting.

You may question what you should expect. At this point in this book, you know that we are going to plan for and expect success in this first meeting. Let's simply plan for success and have what has happened up to now be the foundation for your success. If you plan for success and set yourself up for success, you will create a space to succeed.

Notice that negative thoughts will arise in your mind. Observe those negative thoughts and practice letting them go. The thoughts you focus on will create associated thoughts. Practice letting go of negative thoughts. This will create the space for you to observe the thoughts arising, and if they are not thoughts you want to focus on, you can learn to let the negative thinking go.

As I have said in previous chapters, this is a learned process. If you were to notice that you were brought up focusing on the negative, it will take work to implement adjusting your mind to see the negative thoughts arise and learn to let them go. You may have to take physical action to assist yourself to let them go.

Doing activities like going for a walk, doing some quick exercises or simply moving your body to assist your mind to learn to let go of the negative thinking.

To best prepare, you ultimately will set up a plan for success. Preparation will create the foundation for success. In the workbook, there are some exercises associated with this chapter. The workbook can be found at: www.PeacefulFamilyDynamics.com/Workbook. You can download the online workbook here.

Reflect upon your intention for the relationship; it will assist your mind in creating a foundation of empowered possibility. As you dwell in this possibility in what could happen, you will create and live in a mindset of positivity.

In this mindset of positivity, you will be confident and self-assured. Remember, if the online meeting went well, it set the stage for the in-person meeting to go well.

If the online meeting went just okay, it is time to step up your preparation to have the face-to-face meeting go better.

Confidence is an inside job, as described in the earlier chapter on the 10 Cs. You may want to review your intention and the positive interactions that have occurred up to now. Reflecting upon these will create the space of self-assurance as you prepare to meet face to face.

You can expect a level of nervousness in the first meeting. This is quite normal. And acknowledging the nervousness is the best way to shift your mind away from being nervous into a space of calm — possibly even having a good time.

If you notice you are nervous, take a deep breath. You may want to take a number of deep breaths that will break the nervousness. If you have nervous habits, be aware of them. If they begin, simply be aware. If you already have ways you let go of nervousness, do those. It may be valuable to talk about nervousness in the conversation. I promise the other person is probably nervous and will understand.

It is best to find a neutral space where both parties feel comfortable for the initial face-to-face meeting. For this first meeting, plan to meet at a café or a coffee shop.

The atmosphere will give both of you the opportunity to feel more comfortable. You may consider asking the other person if they have a favorite place to meet.

You may worry about not being mentally prepared. Chances are low that you won't be mentally prepared. If you have read this book and done the exercises, you will be prepared. Notice when fear arises. By now you have been doing exercises where you are learning to let go of the fear and step into a space of peace.

Creating a checklist will assist you in preparing for success. If the virtual meeting went well, chances are the face-to-face meeting will also go well. Mentally review what worked up to date. Continuing to focus on the positive will create the mindset where it will continue to be a positive interaction.

Review your checklist. If you feel the need to adjust or modify it, this is the perfect time. This is a living document; you can modify it as the relationship grows.

Allow for an easy out so both parties are comfortable ending the meeting in the very unlikely event someone gets overwhelmed. Know that it is quite normal to be nervous during the meeting. Acknowledge your nervousness by briefly mentioning it to create the space for it to be minimized.

In the highly unlikely event it ends early for an unknown reason, discuss how to best communicate moving forward. In today's busy world, something may arise that causes the meeting to end early. That does not mean anything unless you make it mean something. Planning to reconnect is the best way to move beyond an unforeseen situation.

Dress for confidence; do everything you can to feel confident. Select clothes that you are comfortable in, maybe your favorite clothes, or clothes that help you feel confident. Select clothes that are neutral and do not make any strong statements. You may want to review Chapter 7 and that section of the workbook.

As was discussed in an earlier chapter, confidence is a created state. As you have planned and know your goals and intentions, chances are after the first few minutes of nervousness, the confidence will arise and the meeting will be wonderful.

Chances are better than average the meeting will be wonderful!

9

SELF-REFLECTION

"People who have had little self-reflection live life in a huge reality blind-spot."
— Bryant McGill

This chapter is about self-reflection and you. As a result of the developing relationship, thoughts may arise inside your mind. We will reflect and focus on the potential "stories" that arise inside your mind. You will most likely do some journaling after you answer some common questions and reflect. Getting close to someone also means getting closer to yourself and developing a deeper understanding of who you are.

The greatest benefit available to you in the space of self-reflection is empowerment and self-growth. Both of these will, as an indirect result, strengthen the bond you are creating with your new relative. Human growth can be a wonderful thing.

As the relationship develops, you may notice issues arise in your mind. Write out the stories you are thinking or seeing in your imagination, how you are feeling, and any other thoughts arising in your mind. Now is the ideal time to deal with and process them to create a better life. As you process your issues, it will open up the space to become mentally and emotionally healthier. As you do this, your life will become clearer and you will experience it from an empowered space.

Once you have written out the issues, you may have to look outward to process them, whether it is with a coach, mentor, therapist, or close friend. If you have professional support, that will be the perfect space to process, as long as the professional is proficient in dealing with the type of issues that arise. If they are outside the professional's area of practice, have them refer you to another professional who can.

If you do not have professional support, you may want to find a coach or mentor that specializes in the area of your issues. Interview a few and find the one that has experience and makes you feel comfortable. Explore free services in your area through community mental health, churches or nontraditional clergy.

You may be a person that reads books to address your deeply rooted issues. You can search out and find books, and do the exercises. Or maybe you have a book club, and possibly a small trusted group can read the same book.

Self-sabotage probably has the greatest potential to damage the new relationship. You may notice thoughts that are moving the relationship backward in your head. One of the first things you can do is write out the thoughts you are having about the relationship. Get them out of your head and out on a piece of paper. When they are on the paper, you can begin to see what you are thinking and possibly let those thoughts go.

You're possibly feeling great, yet you may be wondering when the other shoe is going to drop. This is self-sabotage behavior. Self-sabotage can be a real concern. If you have a track record of self-sabotage, seek professional assistance to have you process and heal through it. Note that this may take effort and time beyond a few sessions.

If you have a number of items, they may seem similar; allow each one to have its own page. Journal about the youngest time you can remember each one happening. Journal about how this behavior has played out throughout your life. The more you write out these similar events, the easier and quicker you can process them.

Once you have written about it, consider processing them with someone you trust. Self-processing is difficult; you are attempting to heal yourself with the same mind that has you creating and living in the situation. Someone else can give you a different viewpoint, and can speed processing. This person should be a professional that specializes in providing you external support to assist you through issues that arise.

This new relationship may have you wanting to foster a deeper sense of self love inside you, toward you. The relationship has the potential to deepen your ability to like, accept and love yourself. Initially, you may see the areas of your life where things are not working, or where similar issues have arisen in the past. As suggested above, write out all of these situations. Get them out of your head and onto a piece of paper or your digital journal. Once out of your head, consider professional support to process them.

This is the space to journal about the good feelings that are arising as a result of the new relationship. Giving some focus to the positive things arising out of the relationship is a way to increase your internal confidence.

This is also the time to explore how to go from good to great with the relationship. List out the good things happening. By focusing on the good things, you can develop an action plan to take them from good to great! As you list these out, simply continue to do the things that are working. Reflect and write out what is working. You are succeeding. Know you can continue to succeed. Have your actions match your success.

If you are struggling, it is time to seek support from the appropriate people to address your concerns. It is very difficult to process and heal yourself. Books may provide the guidance to heal, but seeking external support most likely will be a quicker and more efficient method to process the drama and trauma that may arise. Whether it is a therapist, a coach, or a mentor, select someone to assist you to grow and develop into the best person you can be.

Unresolved trauma may rear its ugly head as the relationship develops. Again, list out all the thoughts and issues that arise. Even if you feel they are minor, write them out. The more you get them out of your head and into a journal, the clearer your mind can become.

If the relationship has struggled, past relationship issues may arise in your thinking. It is quite normal (and may be another shade of self-sabotage). Writing out your stories of failures will assist you to process them and create positive growth.

Healing this will create the space for all areas of your life to improve.

In the event things are going well, returning to your intentions will allow you to focus on growing the things that are working and take your success to the next level.

In the associated workbook, you have some exercises associated with this chapter. The workbook can be found at: www.PeacefulFamilyDynamics.com/Workbook. The link to get the workbook is here.

10

EXPLORING RELATIONSHIP BONDS

"In healthy development, trust evolves. How do we decide whether to trust? We share a feeling with someone and watch their reaction; if the response feels safe, if it is caring, noncritical, non-abusive, the first step of trust has developed. For trust to grow, this positive response must become part of a relatively reliable pattern... Trust develops with consistency over time."
— E. Sue Blume

This is a great time for a relationship assessment. It will allow you, and possibly your new relative, to see where the relationship is and possibly have both parties decide where they would like the relationship to go.

It will begin by asking yourself (and eventually them) how you feel about how the relationship is progressing so far. If you both assess the relationship, you will both be able to see where the relationship is at that moment.

In the workbook, there are some exercises associated with this chapter. The workbook can be found at: www.PeacefulFamilyDynamics.com/Workbook. You can download the online workbook here.

You may feel scared if the relationship seems to be struggling and you are not sure why. As discussed in Chapter 9, mental self-sabotage may be creating fear in your mind. It is natural to fear the relationship may be struggling. Doing a relationship assessment will help you see if your fears are real or created. If after the assessment, you see that you are creating fears that simply are not there, the best move would be to get outside support to heal this.

You may feel that the relationship can be better than this. If so, it simply may be mini-self-sabotage behavior showing up. Relationships can always be better. Part of the assessment may show you where you can enhance improvement in the relationship. As you review the assessment, you likely will see areas of potential growth.

If there is an area of growth, you can develop an action plan to address it. And if it is something you both see, you can co-create growth. Doing this together is one of the strongest ways to create genuine, lasting growth.

If you both agree to take the quiz, it may become apparent where the relationship is struggling. If you both see an area of struggle, see if you can talk about it, and together, grow through it.

If neither of you took the quiz, this may be a little more challenging. And it may be a sign that there is a higher level of struggle in the relationship. Depending upon the level of communication in the relationship, struggle may mean you give the relationship a break.

A break will allow both of you to reflect and assess what you would like to create in the relationship. Breaks are not a bad thing, and the break may have the result of ultimately strengthening the relationship. It may also signal the end or minimization of the relationship. This is a possibility. If the relationship does dwindle, make sure you leave open the possibility of readdressing it in the future. If things change in the future, they will feel comfortable reaching out.

Maybe the relationship is going well, but you feel *you* are struggling. If you have taken the quiz listed above, you may have read the results and found you feel like you are struggling. This can be normal. Take a break and reflect upon why you are struggling. Write it out. Take it to someone you can work out the struggle with. When you work with another person, you can more quickly come to understand the depth of your frustration.

If you have written out your points of struggle, give it a break for a few hours to a day. After the break, come back and assess the struggle. What thoughts and emotions are underneath the struggle? This might be an opportunity to get external support. As there are so many possible areas of struggle, it is best processed once you have written out the struggle. Getting clarity is key to transforming the struggle, or at minimum learning to live with it.

If the other person is open to a conversation about the struggle, come to the conversation in the space of peace and love. Accept what they are saying. They are expressing their struggles with the hope of you hearing what they are saying. Hear them and do your best to *not* make what they are saying mean something about you. These are struggles they are dealing with. Hearing them just might be the most powerful thing you can do.

At this point, one of the possibilities for the relationship is that they do not want the level of relationship you are seeking. You may have some grief and struggle with this. The best idea here is to have patience in the awareness that the speed of the relationship development may slow quite a bit.

If they are requesting a break, accept the request and make sure they know you will be there if they ever change their mind. Be gracious and honor the space. And make sure you have a support network to assist you moving forward.

For a number of reasons, you may not want to develop the level of relationship that the other person wants. The other person may struggle with your decision. Be aware that this may change over time. Have an open conversation with the other person; tell them how you feel. Do this gently, especially if they really wanted to develop the relationship. Leave it with the possibility that if things change in the future, you will reach out.

If you both are choosing to move the relationship forward, have an open conversation about where the relationship is right now and how you would like it to grow. If you both agreed to do the quiz, as you review the results together, you can have a conversation to take the relationship where you both would like it to go. If you have this conversation, that in itself will help take the relationship to the next level.

As a result of the quiz, and if you discuss the results, it will open up the opportunity for each of you to provide feedback on the relationship. Write out the questions you would like to ask. See if you can word them in a neutral or very gentle way. Ask questions in a neutral way, use "I" statements; avoid using "you" questions or comments.

Open the dialogue to make sure no pressure exists on the expectations, especially the "unspoken" expectations. If you cannot have an open conversation, you can determine the parameters, or the rate of communication, which can define the parameters of the relationship.

As you create a path for growth, now would be a good time to review your intentions. Congratulations on the steps you've taken. You both are growing. If you are ready for more, this might be the time to go to the workbook and do the work associated with this section. The workbook can be found at: www.PeacefulFamilyDynamics.com/Workbook.

11

DEEPENING NEW RELATIONSHIPS

"Treat your relationship as if you are growing the most beautiful sacred flower. Keep watering it, tend to the roots, and always make sure the petals are full of color and are never curling. Once you neglect your plant, it will die, as will your relationship."
— Suzy Kassem

By this point, things are most likely going great! We are going to explore moving the relationship forward and deepening the bond along the way. Can you accept where the relationship is? Acceptance is one of the most powerful feelings you can create. Accept the relationship exactly where it is.

Right now, the relationship can be in one of three places:

It may be going great. It is growing and nurturing into a healthy and wonderful relationship.

It may be going neutral. It's neither good nor bad. It is simply there. You may communicate at a time frame and maybe just simple texts. Hopefully the door has been left open so if things change, communication may be opened up in the future. Neutral is simply that: the possibility for communication.

It may have "gone out of" communication. One side or the other has decided not to move the relationship forward at this time. Communication may have slowed or stopped. What began as a possibility is now a closed chapter at this time. Hopefully the space has been left in such a way that if things change in the future, communication can be reestablished. Can you accept this? You may need external support if communication has ceased.

If things are going neutral, good, or great, keep doing what you are doing. It is working. The intentional effort you have been putting into the relationship is working.

Keep those actions and behaviors that have been working going.

All relationships go through phases as they grow. Sometimes the time is great and at other times not so much. If you would like to read a recommended book about relationships, I recommend "The Relationship Handbook" by George Pransky.

In the event the relationship is not meeting your expectations, can you make peace with it? It takes two to build and nurture a relationship. You may not know or understand what is going on in the mind of the other person. Finding peace and a level of acceptance is critical.

In the associated workbook, you have some exercises associated with this chapter. The workbook can be found at: www.PeacefulFamilyDynamics.com/Workbook. The link to get the workbook is here.

You may have mental things arising inside you that are creating turmoil inside you and you may not understand. If this is happening, do not become harsh with yourself. One of the most powerful things you can do is to develop compassion with yourself around the turmoil.

Keep growth going if it is going well. One of the greatest joys is having the relationship grow. You both may develop an empowered and wonderful relationship. Whatever you are doing that is working, continue to do that. And learn to enjoy this new relationship. You may also be moving into a phase where you are both meeting new relatives and developing bonds outside of yourself.

As the relationship develops, doing an ongoing evaluation is a healthy thing to do. If the other person has done the evaluation earlier, they may be open to maybe doing another one maybe once per year. Once you have met and things are going well, continue to plan times to talk and events to deepen the relationship.

What are some of the actions you can do to co-create the relationship with the other person? You may even want to sit down and talk about this with the other person. Together you can co-create actions and ways to deepen the relationship. You may even plan a vacation or time together so each of you can become a better version of yourself.

Now would be a great time to reflect on the other chapters, and possibly review a chapter. It also might be a great time to reflect on your goals and intentions. As the relationship develops, your intentions will grow and change.

You may even recommend the other person read this book. It will give you both a common resource to talk about and some common exercises to work through. One of the greatest practices we can implement is to ongoingly mentally grow.

If you are keeping the joy going, the new relationship may open the space to take your life to the next level. This will enrich your life and the lives you impact as a result. Hopefully this book has assisted you in an empowering way.

Thank you for creating the space as a result of implementing the knowledge in these chapters! Thank you for the effort you are putting into your life.

12

HEALING INNER WOUNDING

I began coaching in 2002, and started a full-time career as a Life Architect in December 2005. Since 2008, my focus has been on addiction recovery, trauma and the human condition. I have conducted workshops for more than 30,000 people in addiction recovery centers and have worked with hundreds of individual clients.

It's time to look within and potentially resolve your early mental and emotional wounding! Every human has wounding that occurs as a simple result of being human and the way we experience our life in the early years.

I define trauma as a situation that is *not* of love that creates a lasting negative impact on your experience of life. Traumas are responses to events that we carry forward with us in life, and as a result some people's lives are deeply affected, while other people seem to negotiate life in spite of their trauma.

Your original trauma occurred when you were very young, most likely before the age of 5. This trauma is what I call your first break from the original love each child is born with. This event has you experience the first not-of-love feeling in life.

This break from love is the foundation and beginning of your negative emotions in your life (a very simple "core story" you gave yourself).

As a result, this core story subconsciously drives (runs) you in that which is not-of-love in your life. I use the term not-of-love to describe that which is *not* love. I have found that describing that which is *not* of the emotion in question is universally understood. This is not the opposite of the emotion, it is that which is simply *not* the emotion.

When I'm working with my clients we determine their original break from love (your core story) and how it impacted their life all the way to the point we began our work together.

Each human being experiences trauma and drama at some level throughout their life. Some handle it far better while others are deeply impacted by it throughout life. The more you understand your trauma and the roots of your trauma, the easier it becomes to navigate the life you create and live into.

For you, I'd simply ask you to ponder your early upsets and accept that there is an original trauma that drives the "Shadow" side of your being. This book is not intended to dive into shadow work; there are many wonderful people who have created books and programs around shadow work.

The discovery of a biological relative often may trigger strong and deep feelings. I believe this discovery is, at some level, another possible "trauma" you are experiencing. Have you noticed that this discovery triggered your inner wounding that came about as a result of early trauma?

My term for the traumas we experience through life is: a significant emotional event. A significant emotional event can be positive or negative, trauma that we hold on to long after the experience. We tend to remember the negative significant emotional events and those tend to have a deeper impact on our experiences in life. Our early significant emotional events tend to grow up with us and impact us until we do the work to understand them and possibly, heal them.

When I first learned about this, it made a lot of sense. At

one point, I listed out my significant emotional events. Oftentimes, you will have experienced many significant emotional events in your life. And you have to understand that it is the stories we create around our significant emotional events that deeply impact our experience in this space of how we create this thing we call life!

As you come to understand your life experience, especially as you become aware of the impact of these significant emotional events, almost as the filter or lenses that impact the story you create inside your mind about life. There are many paths to understanding, one of the ways we will explore opening your awareness and understanding is through meditation. Take a moment, close your eyes, allow your thoughts to flow down the river of thought, and clear your mind.

Begin to take a deep breath, and accept that you had a significant emotional event (over time, complete this exercise for each significant emotional event). If you meditate, sit quietly and allow the emotion and the thought about this new event to rise up. Open your eyes and write down the thought and the emotion. Even if it sounds silly, write it down. Do this for as long as it takes to have the thoughts and emotions go from your head to a piece of paper. If you have someone to assist to process each one, oftentimes that is the quickest way to understand.

Maybe you have not learned how to meditate. Sit quietly and ponder the thoughts and stories going through your head. Either write these thoughts out on paper or type them out on a computer. See the thoughts written out. What if things aren't as they seem? Understand that THIS is how you feel as a result of this discovery. Again, this would be the time to get an external person to assist you to process the impact of these events.

The deeper you understand, the clearer your mind becomes. The clearer your mind is, the easier it is in life to be happy, joy filled, and create an amazing life. At the end of the day, isn't creating an amazing experience of life?

In the space of creating an amazing life, the discovery of another biological relative can be created from a place of joy and love. Whether you create a lifelong bond or not, using the exercises in this book will greatly increase the probability of finding joy and love in life! The workbook can be found at: www.PeacefulFamilyDynamics.com/Workbook. You can download the online workbook here.

13

PARENT(S) OTHER THAN THE ONES YOU KNOW

Maybe you have suspected that one or both of the parental units that raised you were not your biological parents. Possibly you have done a DNA test and found out the parent(s) who raised you are not your biological parents.

It might also be something obvious like your birth certificate does not have a name in one of the boxes, or you simply have a gut feeling.

When you find a biological match, it is time to do the work. Being able to create an empowering relationship is the reason this book was written.

After you read the below shared stories people wrote for me to share, go through the exercises in the earlier part of the book, take the quiz and do the exercises. This will give you the greatest probability for you to create an empowered relationship. Patiently choose to create an empowering relationship with your new discoveries. You can do this empowered!

Greg's story
Finding his biological father

I first began searching for my bio dad when I was 13. I knew his name but couldn't find anything about him. I later found out I was spelling his name incorrectly. When I was 18, a social worker knew that if my dad was a pit boss at a casino, he would have had to be licensed through the local police department. We were able to find him through this process. My initial feeling was excitement and hope.

The initial meeting was stressful. My dad is a pretty easy-going guy who has worked with at-risk youth for years, so he handled it gracefully and with kindness. We have developed a good relationship and speak often. At times we have strains, but overall it is good; I am happy to know him. I feel good about it. I often wish I knew him when I was younger, but I am glad we met when we did.

Managing expectations going into a new relationship with a bio parent is important. I often was so disappointed because of the 18 years of imagining what my dad was like that created this perfect version of him in my mind, and when he failed to be that, I would be frustrated. If you want a relationship, it's important to find a way to grieve the childhood you lost, and forgive the bio parent for not being around.

I have learned to deal with lots of cognitive behavior therapy. I went through a book about the potential loss before I met him in case I really may have had to let him go, so I think I was prepared to meet him because I had already worked through losing the man who raised me. After meeting him, trying really hard to understand where he came from, and what his situation was like made it easier to see the good person behind the mistakes.

We have developed a good relationship and speak often.

Dale's story
Discovering his biological father

I first discovered I had a different father than the father who raised me when I was about 18 or 19. I was visiting my grandmother. She brought out a box of old photos and I recognized one of my mother when she was young. I was confused because she was in a wedding dress, but the man next to her was not my present father. As well, I saw a physical resemblance to myself in that man. I asked who the man was next to my mom, she said it was my father. My grandmother was unaware that this had been kept from me. I told her my birth certificate stated the current father was my father. She explained to me that back I was adopted by the man who raised me, with a new birth certificate issued with the adopted father's name.

Initially I was distrustful of my mother and stepfather for keeping this secret from me. Then I got curious about discovering who and where my biological father was and I pondered if I should initiate contact.

I did not find his contact information until I was about 26 or 27. I initiated contact through the phone at first. My biological father and his wife were very happy and excited that I made contact. We had phone conversations over the next six months, then agreed to a meeting at his home. There my sister and I (we were both his children) met him and two half brothers and four half sisters. Both my biological dad and our new stepmom attempted to make it a celebration. Pictures were taken with the whole family as introductions were made.

After that initial meeting, my biological dad and stepmom continued to engage with us. My sister was not as comfortable with the connection. As well, there was a variation of different feelings appearing with the half-siblings. The oldest boy and girl seemed uncomfortable at times, most likely because most of their life they were the oldest and now learned they were not.

My father and stepmom continued to have an ongoing relationship with my family and me, up to their passing a few years ago. When my father learned he had cancer and would pass soon, I was one of the first he called. My half siblings that are still alive and I have some contact, except for those who have passed. We all seemed to like and be comfortable in their new role as aunt or uncle to my children even up to now. They seem to connect more with my children these days. I went into this discovery initially with no expectations and let what happens happen. I have peace with the whole situation today.

One strange fact: When I had that first meeting, I discovered that my biological dad and stepdad only lived four blocks from each other without knowing it. Later, when my stepdad retired from the Army, he bought a house way out in the country by a lake. Around that same time my biological dad's mother passed, she left them some family land and he moved out to this family land. It was only a few miles from my step dad's place. Ironic, isn't it?

14

YOU ARE A BIO-DAD

The minute you find out you have a biological child you've never met, the first thing you should do is to simply let the shock set in.

You either expected this, or this was a total surprise. First, sit down and take a deep breath, maybe 20 deep breaths.

Either you have discovered you are a father for the first time or you have discovered another biological child. Most likely you have not raised the new discovery, yet fate and DNA testing have verified you are now the biological father of a person that before the discovery, was not in your world.

When you initially find your discovery, it may be by an email stating you have a father/child match, or possibly you have received a message from someone who through DNA testing, or a family member doing DNA test, suspects they are related to you.

Reflect upon the impact on your life.

One of two scenarios is unfolding:

You are the one reaching out. This most likely is a wonderful surprise. You are in anticipation of a response. Once you have chosen to reach out, the next best move is patience. Once the other person has received the message, they may have to ponder how to respond and even if to respond. Step into a space of patience.

Someone has reached out to you. In this instance, you may be in a space of surprise, shock, denial, or unsurety. It is time for you to reflect upon the information. When my sister first reached out, I was in complete denial. It took the results from the DNA test I took for me to acknowledge I indeed had a previously unknown son, and that he was actually my biological son.

The discovery of the author's son

One of the first things that came up in my initial message once the discovery was made was the question about whether I knew (remembered) the mother. In my instance, I had no real memory of the mother. Once the mother sent a picture, after 37 years I had a faint recollection of her. She called within an hour of me giving my number to my son. Unlike me, his mother remembered everything — where we met, where we had gone on the two dates we had, and that we had been intimate (my words, not hers) once. And then she said in a very harsh voice, "And you never called me back."

My commitment moving forward was to begin to build a relationship with my newly found son.

Building a relationship from discovery

Building a relationship takes time, effort, patience, and more time. The older the newly discovered offspring is, the slower building the relationship will most likely take. Remember, just because you have a biological relationship does not guarantee building the relationship will be easy. And as you build the relationship, it will go through times where the communication is flowing, other times it will go ever so slowly.

The main thing to remember is slow and steady. Especially around holiday times. The offspring may have been anticipating this moment, yet when it actually hits, it most likely will be far more difficult than imagined. Around holidays, they may become more distant, simply giving your offspring the time and space to adjust to their newly discovered biological father.

Consider that you do not know what the humans who raised the child communicated about the child's origins. This may be a complete shock. Without a doubt, they have created a story inside their head about what you should be like, and you may, or may not, meet that expectation.

I cannot express enough the importance of going slow and steady and taking deep breaths in and out as the relationship develops. Develop a friendship, then deepen the friendship into family. Slow, steady, and forward is the path to be implemented. If you go "too fast," you may push this new and important relationship away instead of bringing you closer.

One of the first questions to ask yourself is what kind of relationship you would like to create with this newly discovered offspring. Reflect and write out your reasons and objectives. Really get clear about what you are creating. Include the people who have raised the child as well.

So what is the intention you would like to achieve in this relationship? Put some thought into what you are beginning to create. Write it out. Write out every possible intention, set the writings down for a bit. Return to review what you have written and see which ones rise to the top. Choose the top intention and have that be your intention you create in every interaction.

Being aware of your intention as you continue to develop the relationship will take surprise out of the journey. It will give you the ability to develop a solid relationship with your newly discovered human.

The author's story on this:

I would not have found my son had a DNA test not verified a story in my family for most of my life.

When I was a child, my other sister and I listened outside my parent's bedroom while my mother was intimate with men other than my father. The youngest sibling was different from the other three kids.

As kids, our teasing was merciless. Teasing her and telling her to go ahead and ask our parents and asking her, "Do you think they will tell you the truth?"

Fast forward to 2020. My youngest sister and I ended up buying DNA kits for each other and taking the tests. On a Sunday afternoon she called me and said she had gotten her results back, and there had been a mistake. We were listed as half-siblings. I was a bit surprised and said it was accurate. I asked her if anyone else had talked to her, because we (the other siblings and my father) had been talking about this for years. I discovered that no one else had told her what we all had known all along.

15

YOU ARE ADOPTED

So you are adopted, and have found, or are seeking to find your biological parents.

This book will help you create an empowered communication once you find your biological parents.

Reflecting back prior to the 1980s and before, getting information on your birth origins was almost impossible. Yet since that time, laws have changed such that it is becoming much easier to locate the information and have a higher chance of finding your biological parents.

And the rapid growth of DNA testing also increases the chances of you finding your biological parents.

The advantage of learning about the 10 Cs discussed in Chapter 1 and applying them is that you get the opportunity to create a relationship anew, free from the constraints created by your past relationships.

Chapter 12 of this book deals with the inner wounding you dealt with growing up.

Oftentimes if you have been adopted, you may feel "thrown away." This potentially creates a deep inner wound. And when you find your biological parents, you often learn the actual reason is quite different from what you created in your mind.

Biological parents commonly have deep regret about what happened. A percentage of the time people may also find out the biological father may have never known the mother was pregnant with you.

And from the point of discovery, you have potential to create a relationship that empowers all involved.

Lynda's story of being adopted

My adopted name is Lynda Elizabeth T. I have always known I was adopted. My first boyfriend in high school actually helped me find this long after we broke up. And he found his birth family and informed them of what happened with my adoption. I had never wanted to find my birth family but Mark (my husband now) wanted me to. I am glad I did. They are more family than I could wish for.

In 2014 I found out about my birth family. When my first husband and I were Immigrating to the USA, US immigration told me I needed my adoption order. I asked my parents for it and they refused. I requested a copy from the court and it was sent. It arrived and sat on our mantle for quite a while. I had my husband look at it first. Then I opened it. It had my birth mother's name on it: Phyllis Margaret M. And my birth name: Heather Lee M. I had always liked the name Heather and I now know why my parents didn't really call me Margaret.

It was not until my dad passed and my mother was already forgone with Alzheimer's that I wrote to the Canadian State Government to release my name if anyone was looking for me. The government sent me all of my adoption papers. My friend then took those and looked on a DNA site and found my older 1/2 sister (that was determined later through another DNA test with another company) and that led to finding my whole birth family.

I met my younger sister when she first came to my oldest son's wedding. The next year she came to Burning Man and volunteered. I then went home to Alberta/British Columbia to attend my oldest sister's retirement party. I met the whole family. At one point, when we went to pick up one of our Beagles, I met Auntie Heather, who I am named after. I look like the aunt and very much like her daughter who, unfortunately committed suicide. I have a good relationship with the family. I am not the first adopted person. There is one other male who found the family about 10 years before me.

I'm also in regular communication with two aunts now. I am social media friends with the rest of the family. When I go home to Canada, we meet. It is not close to besties but we visit. I am not considered an outsider, I am family. My two sisters have bigger relationship problems with each other. I have developed my own relationship with each of them.

I am glad I was adopted. I grew up with a better situation. I would have had an abusive family had I not been adopted. Alcoholic and more. This is why I do not drink anymore. Listening to stories, my birth mum grew up poor and things didn't get much better. I had a very middle-class upbringing and lived in Europe for two years. My parents were not abusive.

I am a good example of Nature vs. Nurture: I walk like my sisters; I hold a Kleenex in my hand like my adopted mum; I am the same height as my birth mum and look like her; I hold my hands up like my adopted mum.

16

NEW SIBLING(S)

There is a wonderful beauty in discovering you have siblings previously unknown. You have the potential to develop an empowered relationship with someone who shares some level of DNA with you. And right now, you both have a blank slate in creating a relationship.

If you could get any benefits for your life out of creating a relationship, what would they be? Think about what you can create and write it down.

As you begin to write, what are the desires, wishes, and values you bring to the relationship? How have relationships gone for you up to date? What do you desire as a result of the relationship? Think of this from the perspective of the new sibling. What are the great and wonderful qualities you bring to this burgeoning family?

If you have self-doubts and stories about the past that cloud your potential greatness, now is the time, place and space to let them go. These new relationships are your opportunity to step into your greatness

Wes' story of finding a biological brother

I found my brother on my father's side. He went on a sorority date with her one time and that's the only time they met. I found out through Facebook, which was embarrassing. I was 43 years old when I found out. My initial reaction was shock. My father was shocked.

My half brother and I started to create a relationship at first through the computer. Once we started to talk, I could tell we were completely different from each other. He played computer games his whole life and I was always into physical activities such as sports. I haven't spoken to him since he and his wife went through a divorce. We have not met. I doubt we ever will.

I could have lived my whole life without knowing he existed. Understand, I had a little brother that died when he was 20. That's the only brother I relate to. I guess my expectations were to slowly build up a relationship to see where it would go. At one time I figured we'd end up meeting and have a distant relationship. Right now I'm personally just fine without him in my life. Again, he hasn't returned two messages I left him a year ago so I assume he doesn't want a relationship. I had hopes of this relationship replacing my brother. That never happened.

I would like to share that I'm a unique person who thinks out of the box. The really weird thing is we are both alcoholic and we're both married to red haired, blue eyed women. I would like to add: blood isn't always blood.

I haven't found inner peace at all. Sometimes I feel like I should be at peace, and I am currently very comfortable with my life. I feel he brings drama to my now undramatic life. I chose peace in my life, so he is not really active in my life.

Alicia's story of discovering a half brother

Twenty seven years ago, I found my half brother John. I'm so happy and love him very much!

When you find a biological relative, don't go in expecting anything. They don't owe you and you don't owe them. Keep it chill and just find out more about each other if you want to.

Since daddy died when I was 10 (John was 5), John's mom and my father never married and she never initiated contact with my mom, we simply didn't know each other. John had left home at 16; I was newly married at 21.

We met because John contacted our Granddaddy Ernie. We all met at a local Mexican restaurant. I was very curious about John and his life. I loved him because he was another connection to our dad. I wanted to know more about John! I was in awe of how much he looked like our dad, Mark Pehkonen. I was relieved that I wasn't crazy, because I had seen him driving in my neighborhood and thought he was my dad — knowing my dad had passed 11 years prior.

We have a relationship but we don't talk as often as I'd like. It has been hard at times because I can sometimes make him feel weird. He is so much like my dad, sometimes I cry when he does normal things like the way he holds his hands, stands, gestures, and facial expressions. It makes John uncomfortable and I try to respect that. It just catches me off guard sometimes and I have to take a minute. I simply miss my dad so very much.

We have grown to love and trust one another but we are not super close. We have created a bond, yet it's casual between us. We are both introverted and know that the other likes to spend time at home after being around a lot of other people. We definitely trust one another. Our children grew up spending the night at each other's houses. My youngest child and his second child are close and still spend time together.

I'm thankful that Granddaddy introduced us to one another. Now we take each other as we are and don't expect or demand anything from each other. Yet I love him just because he is my brother and he has become a good friend.

Sarah's story of discovering biological siblings

My mother didn't marry my father, but brought me up on her own in England. My father was already married in an arranged marriage in Iraq. He already had five children before he met my mother, then after their affair he went back to Iraq and had a few more. I am in the exact middle of his nine children, three girls and six boys. Actually, I always knew I had these biological half siblings, but I didn't meet them until 2014, when I was age 57.

I always thought my father had abandoned me and didn't care about me at all. In 2015, I found a trove of his letters in my mother's things (she died in 2009) and in the letters he expressed his side of the story, he cared about me and wanted me to be with him. This was immensely healing for me, to realize he had loved me all along.

Meeting my siblings was amazingly warm and welcoming! I had just lost my mother, and our father had died many years earlier. I met around 20 of my relatives for the first time, including brothers, sisters, cousins, nephews and nieces. They came from all over Iraq. I met them in Kurdistan, which was relatively safe at that time. I stayed there just three days. They showered me with gifts and affection.

It was amazing, because I've always been an "only child" with just a mother, no father, so now I feel like I'm part of an actual family, even though I can hardly ever see them in person. I am thrilled that I finally met them and discovered a little about myself too, because I never knew my father. They say I am "like him" in looks and temperament. I am closest with my sister Dapne, who is the matriarch of the family and keeps in touch often.

The main challenge we all face is that my sisters and brothers are in Iraq and so it's very difficult for us to connect in person, although we did manage to do so once. My sister keeps asking me to visit again, but it's not that easy, and she can't leave the country to visit me.

Not only are these people my family, they are also Arab, Muslim and from a very alien culture to me (brought up in England and spent most of my life in America, typical white Christian). And yet they are so like me, and we have a connection that goes much deeper than these superficial things. I think it would be great to write a book sometime about my experience.

17

MET A DISTANT RELATIVE

In this new world of DNA discoveries, one of the by-products of doing a DNA test is finding distant relatives. Great opportunities for expanding your circle exist if you explore your relatives after a DNA test. Although the other possibility exists for you to find someone through a mutual friend's FaceBook page.

As you begin to create relationships, the steps in the first part of the book are important as you have the potential to grow your list of relatives and expand your circle of influence.

At times, these relative discoveries may not be earth shattering to you, you will still find incredibly cool people that are your relatives. And it is quite possible to develop these relationships. Teri's story is from a personal friend who found a relative through last names and my social media page.

Teri's story of meeting a distant cousin

My second cousin Jerry and I discovered each other through the author's Facebook page quite coincidentally about 8 years ago. :)

As mutual friends, he noticed my last name on a post comment, which was the same as his mother's maiden name, and reached out on Messenger to see if we could be related. And we were! I believe our grandfathers were brothers (on my father's side).

We met in person about a year later when I flew to Denver for a family function (on my mother's side) and have seen each other several times since then, in person and on-line. I've also met or done video-conference with several of Jerry's siblings.

It's wonderful to be reconnected with a long-lost branch of my family and I look forward to more visits in the future, and introducing them to my aunt and cousins at some point.

18

GAVE UP A CHILD FOR ADOPTION

One of the most difficult things a woman can do is give up a child for adoption. The reasons are many, and the impact tends to be lifelong.

This book is not intended to process the issues that arise out of the decision. The intention is to get you to understand the importance of creating empowered communication once the child potentially has reached out and is seeking to create a relationship.

From the moment that communication has potential of happening again, understanding the 10 Cs of effective communication (in Chapter 1) will allow you to begin to foster an empowered relationship with your child.

If you have the chance to develop an empowered

relationship, what is available for you, the child, and for those in the circle of influence?

Kat's story of finding an adopted daughter

When I was 15, I gave up a baby for adoption. When we found each other, she was 28 and I was about to turn 44. It was a parent/child match on a DNA testing site. I felt shock, relief, fear, amazement and intrigue, in that order.

Shock because I wasn't even searching and didn't even put together in my head that I could find her through a DNA search. It had never dawned on me.

Relief that she was alive and healthy. Fear that she hated me, didn't want to know me, we wouldn't meet and even that she didn't know that she was adopted. This is all the initial feelings with the first two weeks or so leading up to my first message to her.

I didn't want her DNA search to end up being a shock. I was seeking amazement and intrigue because I wanted to know everything I could about her. I googled stalked her as much as I legally could. I later found out she did the same to me. Lol.

I'm elated although it has been a hard road to this point. I needed to educate myself on adoption trauma, distinguish what her boundaries were and respect them while also griev-ing the loss of not raising her, coming to terms with the fact that I will never be her "mother," grieving the 15-year-old me who was forced to relinquish her and a myriad of others things that triggered the complex PTSD that I didn't realize I had. I wouldn't change it for the world because not only did I find my daughter and begin a relationship with her, I also am finding my true self and building a relationship with me.

There is no manual to reunion. There is no guidance. Although every person, situation and reunion is different, there is barely any kind of help at all. Therapy doesn't always include adoption informed counselors, books besides memoirs are almost non-existent, support groups are just becoming more known, YouTube has virtually nothing. What little there is, is old, outdated and doesn't even touch on the mental mindfuck that reunion is.

Reunion isn't easy. Nothing about it is. We met after about 11 months of getting to know each other. The first meeting was nerve wracking as I was meeting her parents and siblings for the first time as well. We have a good, growing and evolving relationship. We meet almost monthly for lunch and text daily, and 2023 will be over four years building a relationship. We are also going on a trip to my home country Hungary this year.

Author's note: Cat has a YouTube channel about adoption reunion and associated trauma:
https://www.youtube.com/@AdoptionReunion

Suzanne's story of giving up her daughter for adoption

I was 26 years old when I got pregnant. I could very well have kept her and done the single mother struggle but I really wanted what was best for her. I explored a lot of possibilities and didn't make a decision until I was six months pregnant. Once I made the decision, I never doubted it was right. Even when the actual time came to let her go, it was so hard. I felt good that she was going to a loving home. Now that we have reconnected, I know that was the best thing to happen.

Obviously, I had wanted a reunion for all of her life but my life choices limited my opportunities. Once I got my life on a good course, I started putting it out in the universe but all the while knowing it would have to be her choice to connect.

Our initial connection via messages was four years ago. Reconnecting has literally brought so much joy into my life. We spent quite a few weeks emailing back and forth with "get to know you" questions. It was a great way to get any uneasiness out of the way. We made a decision to let things be organic and not to force things to happen. Our initial in person meeting was at a restaurant and of course, I got there way early and could not wait for her to arrive. I cried ....

Every time we are together, I am in awe of the woman she is and the mother she is. When we reconnected, I found out that I was a grandma which I never thought would happen. It has been one of the singular greatest events in all my years. She was my first born so having her was joyful but letting her go was hard so finding her was like birth all over again.

19

MET A PARENT LATER IN LIFE

We live in a society where it is very common for a young human to be raised with a single parent. As you can see in the following account, this has an impact. Phoenix bravely wrote a letter and began building a relationship with his biological father in high school.

We all yearn to have healthy and solid relationships with both of our biological parents. If you have been raised by a single parent, you can still go through the steps in this book and create an empowered relationship.

You may even become surprised with a larger and expanded family that you did not expect. Oftentimes you have to let go of the potential anger you are holding on to inside your mind and heart. You may feel abandoned, alone, not cared about, or even thrown away. These are common thoughts that develop as a result of a biological person not being in our life.

You do not know what will happen as you initiate and develop the relationship, yet what is potentially available is a new and empowered relationship.

If you have a parent you have lost a relationship with, take the chance and see if you can create a new friend.

Phoenix's story of reuniting with his father

I met my dad and siblings 37 years ago. Here is my story.

I took a health class my senior year of high school. The class was titled Personal Growth and Motivation. It was taught by the football coach Dee Hawkes who was an amazing individual. To get a grade in the class, we all had to pick something that was out of our comfort zone and write a report about our process. In my case, I elected to write my bio-dad a letter.

At the time I was 18 years old and I was raised as an only child. Just the year before I had really gotten on my mom's case for not having any other children. My parents had divorced when I was 2 years old and the last time I saw my dad was when I was 3. I sent my letter and a few weeks later he wrote me back.

In his letter he told me that I had two sisters and three brothers (all of them have a different mom but same dad). I was very excited as I felt I had just won the lottery and went from being an only child to now the oldest of six! Yahoo! So as soon as I graduated high school, I jumped on an airplane in Seattle (where I was living) and flew to Salt Lake City. I remember being so nervous on the plane. This was back in the day when everyone could go right to the gate. So I wasn't sure exactly who was going to pick me up, but when I got off the plane, there was my gang, dad, stepmom and five siblings. It was a great moment for me as I had never known anyone else who had my same last name, but now I did and I was relieved in my spirit as I felt I had somewhere that I belonged.

One of the things I saw right away was this man, who was my father, who really couldn't tell me a whole lot about how to live my life, because I was already an adult and had been living on my own for a year by then. In my mind there was no pressure of child/parent relationship. Instead I determined that we would start as friends, and that's what we did.

My dad is a very simple man, very stubborn (so is my mom and that means I got a double dose of stubbornness) but very soft spoken. Of course, our relationship has grown. My dad was in construction or maintenance most of his life. It was when I was 26 that I'd say that he and I finally got it right in our relationship. Up until then, for some un-conscious reason, I didn't give a shit about owning tools. I think it was my way of saying "fuck you" for not being there for me.

Consequently, I think I own a screwdriver and maybe a hammer and a pair of pliers and that was it. After he and I got everything correct, my whole world changed in the sense that I started buying tools, and I started actually working on things because I was no longer in rebellion to my relationship with him and the tools and our relationship grew.

However, it was probably 12 years ago that I noticed that both my parents did not do a very good job of acknowledging me as a human being, or any of my talents or skills. I approached my dad and told him that I didn't feel that he took notice of my life very much and asked him if he would do a better job of that, which I am happy to say my dad rose to the occasion. I would say over the last 12 years he and I have talked or FaceTime every week. One of my favorite things in life is when he and I get off the phone with each other, I just have him laughing at his delights of having me in his life and him in my life.

Elizabeth's story of discovering her biological father

My story is still unfolding and I still have healing to do around it. I searched online but always came up empty. I haven't confronted my mother with a lot of what I share below since our relationship is already quite fragile and distant. There are some sensitivities around what my mother told me and what her friend told me that my mother never told my father about me — not until she found him in

2005. I've been processing this for almost a year now. Here is my story:

After many years of growing up without ever knowing or meeting my father, my mother finally located him in 2005 — living in Spain. I was 35 years old and at the time was going through some pretty tumultuous feelings about life. I was very resistant to meeting him. In my mind I figured he had 35 years to look for me. I had moved on with my life, married with three kids, and made a life that did not include him. At this time, I did not contact him.

I was very bitter and resentful. I am still moving through some strange emotions about the whole thing. I had been fine and processed it all since 2005/2006 and then in March of 2022, I had received a phone call from a close friend of my mother, who told me, "I feel that you should know that your mother never told your father about you. He didn't even know about you." What? It was like watching a movie (like Sixth Sense) and you get later in the movie and find out a piece of information and then you go back and replay the past years with this new insight.

So much hurt and anger but yet understanding and compassion filled me. It was like I was experiencing my emotions as well as that of my mother's when I was in her womb and realizing that this man was not being faithful to her (she found him in bed with the mother of my younger brother). She packed up and left him — she was 24 years old and probably scared and unsure of how she was going to make it in a new country now with a baby on the way.

I had compassion for the 24 year old and imagined how I would probably do the same thing. My projected words and thoughts are, "He's dead to me and he will never get to meet this child — he doesn't deserve it." But then as the baby, I felt this blanket of not being wanted and of being "the problem."

I have since found out that while I grew up an only child with my single-mother (she NEVER had another relationship that I know of after him — EVER) that I was not really an only child. I actually am one of seven children that he had. The other six half siblings all come from different mothers — all from different parts of the world: US, Honduras, Spain, Portugal, UK, and Argentina. Those are the ones that we know of to date. There may be more — who knows. My father has passed.

The discovery of siblings has been lovely — yet I could probably do a better job of being connected to them. I am closest to my older brother who I feel some kind of connection with. He is someone I am so grateful for. In a way I feel like I'm learning about myself through him. I opened up to him whilst I was visiting him in the UK and he smiled and told me, "You know that's how our family line is — we're like race horses that just keep running and running — and we do it for our family and we do it for those that we love — and we'll do it until we run ourselves into the ground, because we don't know anything else ... it's in your genes."

I feel like I'm not alone anymore, that I know more about the mystery that is me. I've lived my life without even knowing much if anything about where I come from on the mother and father sides. So I would say the discovery has been a blessing.

What a strange feeling to not know who I am, to not know the family stories that I could pass down. I'm realizing the importance of preserving these stories —it's a practice that we as tribes would do, what the elders would pass down, the stories and knowledge and wisdom. We have lost this practice and we have lost track of who we are and where we came from.

I'm sure I'm not speaking for all, but stop and think — of the stories you have heard from your parents or even passed down, — how many of those are stories of victimhood? How many are inspirational and uplifting? How many of those are just fun? I grew up hearing the victim stories over and over again (and still do), and it gets tiring to listen to it all. Why are we so scared to tell the stories of when we screwed up and when we were total shits and the silly things we did because we thought we were the best thing since sliced bread? All the things! Why are we so scared to be vulnerable? Our experiences are our nuggets of wisdom that we get to share with others if we so desire — especially with those that share our ancestral blood.

I have contacted the rest of my half siblings who live all across the world. I like to say our father was a busy guy — a renaissance guy who had a lot of charisma and knew how to hustle his way through life. From being an amazing wood-worker carpenter (he came from a family of wood workers), to being an airline pilot, to opening up one of the biggest massage parlors (aka brothel) in New York during the 70s, to running drugs and spending time in prison — our papa really was a rolling stone.

As for my half siblings, I've only met three of them in person. I was planning on going to Argentina in 2020 to meet my oldest brother (our father was 15 years old when he had him) and my younger sister, but that got stopped due to the pandemic and I have yet to reschedule that visit — but I really would like to do that sometime soon. That holds true for my younger brother (three months younger than me) who lives in Honduras.

I have inner peace at this time for the most part. I'm still dealing with letting go of the pain and anger around the new information that surfaced last year. But at this point, how does it serve me to hang on to it? That is what I'm currently working through — as well as feeling guilt for not going and meeting the rest of my siblings. Why do I feel the urge to connect us all? I don't know but I think with time it will surface and I'll understand better.

While I didn't get to meet my father in person, I have de-veloped a relationship with him as he is now in spirit form. He has come through in intuitive mediumship sessions and also plant medicine ceremonies. I hear and feel him with me. In fact, I appreciate having THIS type of relationship with him as opposed to what "could have been." Getting to know more about him and also connecting with him, I understand more of the ancestral karma and wounding that I have been healing within and through me.

20

INVITATION TO MOVE FORWARD

Congratulations on completing the book. Hopefully you are well on the path of creating an empowering relationship with your newly found biological discovery!

In addition to the workbook, YouTube channel, and Facebook page already mentioned, I want to remind you to explore the following resources and opportunities to further support your journey toward creating peaceful family dynamics:

1. Webinars and Workshops: Join my live webinars and workshops where you can deepen your understanding of DNA discovery and gain practical tools to navigate and heal familial relationships. Stay tuned for upcoming events by subscribing to my newsletter.
2. Online Community: Connect with like-minded individuals who have also embarked on this transformative

journey. Join a private online community where you can share your experiences, seek guidance, and receive support from others who understand the complexities of DNA discovery.

3. Individual Coaching Sessions: If you find yourself in need of personalized guidance and support, I offer one-on-one coaching sessions. These sessions provide a safe space for you to explore your unique challenges, address deep-rooted trauma, and develop strategies for fostering peaceful family dynamics.

4. Additional Resources: Explore the recommended reading list, which includes books, articles, and podcasts related to DNA discovery, trauma healing, and relationship dynamics. These resources can further enhance your understanding and provide additional tools for personal growth.

Remember, creating peaceful family dynamics is an ongoing journey that requires patience, self-reflection, and compassionate communication. I am here to support you every step of the way, and look forward to witnessing your continued growth and transformation.

Create an amazing life!

Jim Pehkonen is a Life Architect, a trained and certified Life Coach working with clients experiencing deep trauma and addiction recovery. With over 20 years experience coaching in one-on-one settings and group workshops, he assists his clients in understanding how they create this experience called life. This is his life mission.

In 2003, he began his own transformation, and during the next 10 years of intense experiential study, healed himself first, then grew and developed a coaching business to assist others. He uses a range of healing modalities to support others in their personal transformations.

With his past experience as a general manager in a construction company and trauma recovery coaching in addiction recovery facilities. Jim can help people in all walks of life. This allows him to work with broken businesses to redevelop their team communication, help individuals to connect with themselves, and impact family dynamics so members are able to have more peaceful relationships.

With the discovery of a biological son in 2022, Jim's life has shifted to assisting those seeking to establish effective communication with new biological relatives, and begin writing about healing the trauma that impacts people's ability to live an amazing life.

Realizing that the impact of one-to-one coaching and even workshops was limited to those who could attend in person, Jim stepped into writing so more people like you could be positively affected by his experience, drive and passion.

The website associated with this book can be found at:
www.PeacefulFamilyDynamics.com

The Facebook group associated with this book can be found here.

The link is: https://www.facebook.com/groups/707175597533629.